GW00385222

MEAT

by Gillian Greer

MEAT was first performed at Theatre503, London, on 19 February 2020 and was a finalist in the 2018 Theatre503 International Playwriting Award.

MEAT

by Gillian Greer

Cast

MAX	**India Mullen**
RONAN	**Sean Fox**
JO	**Elinor Lawless**

Creative Team

Director	**Lucy Jane Atkinson**
Designer	**Rachel Stone**
Lighting Designer	**Zia Bergin-Holly**
Sound Designer/Composer	**Annie May Fletcher**
Intimacy/Movement Director	**Adelaide Waldrop**
Stage Manager	**Bryony Byrne**
Production Manager	**Harry Fearnley-Brown**
Assistant Director	**Yusuf Niazi**

Produced by **45North**, **Emily Carewe** and **Theatre503**

CAST

INDIA MULLEN (MAX)

India grew up in Dublin and trained at the Gaiety School of Acting. She is best known for the recurring role of Katie Kiely in the multi-award-winning series *Red Rock* (TV3, BBC). She will next be seen on screen in the BBC adaptation of Sally Rooney's *Normal People*. Her other credits include *Krypton* (Warner Brothers TV and DC) and *Little Women* (BBC), as well as stage work such as the tour of Maeve Binchy's *Light a Penny Candle*, and *The Eurydice Project*.

SEAN FOX (RONAN)

Sean trained at LAMDA, after spending a year at the Bow Street Academy for Screen Acting in Dublin. Since graduating, he has frequented the stage and screen in both the UK and Ireland, most notably in *Jimmy's Hall* directed by Ken Loach, *The Taming of the Shrew* at Shakespeare's Globe, *The Cripple of Inishmaan* at the Gaiety Theatre (Dublin) and *Holby City*. Sean appears as overzealous detective Fitzer in the critically acclaimed crime drama *Taken Down*, set in Dublin's murky twilight world where criminals and slum landlords prey on the vulnerable. It's currently available on BBC iPlayer.

ELINOR LAWLESS (JO)

Elinor trained at the Bristol Old Vic Theatre School where she was awarded the Peter Ackerman Award for Best Comedy Actress. She has also worked as a stand-up comedian, reaching the semi-finals of Amused Moose (Best New Comedy Act) and Laughing Horse (Best New Stand-up). Theatre credits include: *The End of Hope* (Soho Theatre/Orange Tree Theatre); *To Have to Shoot Irishmen*, *Bakkhai* (Almeida Theatre); *King Charles III* (West End); *Terror* (Trinity Theatre); *Stone Cold Murder* (Mill at Sonning); *NewsRevue* (Canal Theatre Café); *The Roaring Girl* (Shakespeare's Globe); *Much Ado About Nothing* (Tobacco Factory); *Hamlet* (Red Rose Chain), *All's Well That Ends Well* (UK tour); *Next Door's Baby*, *Twelfth Night* (Orange Tree Theatre); *Success Story* (Pleasance Theatre/Hen and Chickens). TV credits include: *Flaps* (Comedy Central); *Casualty*, *Doctors*, *EastEnders*, *Shakespeare and Hathaway* (BBC).

ABOUT THE TEAM

GILLIAN GREER (WRITER)

Gillian is a playwright and dramaturg from Dublin who has seen her work performed in The Abbey in Dublin, the Traverse in Edinburgh and all manner of London fringe venues, including Theatre503. Her debut play *Petals* was nominated for the Irish Times Theatre Award for Best New Play in 2015 and was recently adapted for radio. As a dramaturg, she has worked at the National Theatre, VAULT Festival, Clean Break Theatre Company, The Mercury Theatre and many more. She was recently appointed Literary Manager of the Soho Theatre.

LUCY JANE ATKINSON (DIRECTOR)
lucyjaneatkinson.com

Lucy is an experienced and award-winning director. Her work focuses on new writing, incluing musical theatre, devising and immersive theatre. In 2018 she was named Number 1 on The Stage's Top Talents To Watch, stating *'her direction is simple, but acutely sensitive to the shifting energy of the writing. Evident but never overbearing.'*

Recent credits include *A Hundred Words For Snow* by Tatty Hennessy (VAULT Festival/UK tour, Trafalgar Studios; winner: Outstanding New Work, VAULT 2018; 4 Offie nominations including Best Director and Best New Play), and *Vespertilio* by Barry McStay (VAULT Festival, Dublin Fringe; winner: Show of the Week VAULT 2019).

She is currently developing a further host of new plays with an eclectic mix of some of the UK's most exciting up-and-coming playwrights, most notably *Something Awful* by Tatty Hennessy, which opened at VAULT Festival in January 2020.

She is represented by Alexandra Cory at Berlin Associates.

EMILY CAREWE (CREATIVE PRODUCER)
www.emilycarewe.com

Emily has worked in the industry as both an actor and producer since 2013. In 2019 she joined 45North as their Creative Producer for Theatre. Previously, she has worked as a producer for the Royal Philharmonic Orchestra, Sony Music Germany (Audio Drama) and freelance.

Emily is founder and producer of LAMDA MishMash, a festival celebrating the self-created work of LAMDA graduates and their contemporaries taking place for the first time in April 2020, featuring over 25 hours of theatre and film alongside a series of panel talks and workshops.

She trained at LAMDA and The Royal Academy of Music and is a Co-Founder of GEMA Collective– a gender equality movement for actors. www.gemacollective.co.uk

Emily is passionate about new perspectives and voices, inclusivity and giving a platform to people who are often unheard.

RACHEL STONE (DESIGNER)
www.rachelstonedesign.co.uk

Design credits include: *Sweeney Todd, Apologia, Hand to God* (English Theatre Frankfurt); *The Niceties* (Finborough Theatre); *World's End, Boy With Beer* (King's Head Theatre); *Dessert, Stalking the Bogeyman, Upper Cut, Short and Stark* (Southwark Playhouse); *Calamity Jane* (Tring Park School of Performing Arts); *Cabaret* (ACT Aberdeen); *Sweeney Todd* (Twickenham Theatre); *That Face, Carousel* (Landor Theatre); *Songs for a New World, My Mother Said I Never Should* (Bridewell Theatre); *Ruffled* (Theatre503), *Company* (Pleasance Theatre).

Associate credits include: *Handbagged* (UK tour/Roundhouse Theatre Washington/59E59 New York); *Disco Pigs* (Irish Repertory Theatre, New York); *The Grinning Man* (Trafalgar Studios); *Bad Jews* (Arts Theatre); *The EL Train* (Hoxton Hall).

Assistant credits include: *Oedipus Rex, Les Liaisons Dangereuses* (Theatre Cocoon, Tokyo); *Tree* (Young Vic); *Bridges of Madison County* (Menier Chocolate Factory); *True West, Dead Funny* (Vaudeville); *Cendrillon* (Glyndebourne); *Knight's Tale* (Imperial Theatre, Tokyo); *Agrippina, Oliver!* (Grange Park Opera); *The Secret Theatre, The Winter's Tale* (Sam Wanamaker Playhouse); *The Band* (UK tour); *Bat Out of Hell* (Coliseum); *Fatherland* (Royal Exchange Theatre. Manchester); *Watership Down* (Watermill Theatre); *Groundhog Day, The Lorax, Future Conditional* (Old Vic); *The Mentalists* (Wyndham's Theatre); *Anything Goes* (UK tour); *This Is My Family* (Sheffield Crucible); *13* (Apollo Theatre); *Steel Magnolias* (UK tour).

ZIA BERGIN-HOLLY (LIGHTING DESIGNER)
www.ziaholly.com

Zia is an award-winning lighting and set designer. She works internationally and has a base in both London (UK) and Dublin (Ireland). She designs for theatre, dance, opera and live music events.

She is a BA (Hons) graduate of Drama and Theatre Studies, Trinity College Dublin. She went on to participate in the Rough Magic SEEDS Programme 2012–2013 and was the Resident Associate Designer with PAN PAN Theatre 2016–2018.

Her work has included designs for performances as part of the Dublin and Belfast Theatre Festivals, The Dublin Fringe, Vaults London, IPAY, On The Edge, Galway International Arts, Kilkenny Arts, Baboró and 10 Days in Dublin festivals, as well as assistant design credits for performances on the West End.

ANNIE FLETCHER (SOUND DESIGNER)
anniemayfletcher.co.uk

Annie graduated from LAMDA's Technical Theatre & Stage Management FdA course. She is the Laboratory Associate Sound Designer at Nuffield Southampton Theatre 2018/2019 and an Associate Artist with Snapper Theatre company.

BRYONY BYRNE (STAGE MANAGER)

Bryony Byrne is a freelance stage manager working in the UK and abroad. She's worked with the award-winning Wardrobe Ensemble (*Education, Education, Education)* and on the world's longest-running live comedy show, *NewsRevue.* Other work includes *Rachel* (Trestle Theatre), *Derailed* (Little Soldier Productions) and *Our Country* by the experimental LA-based company, Wilderness. She also works with individual artists such as comedian Alison Thea-Skot *(BBC Culture Show)* and Hugh McCann (resident artist at Kaleider). Prior to her stage-management work, she produced and wrote a feature comedy film, *Akela*, which was awarded Best Screenplay at the Vancouver Golden Panda Film Festival. She also performs regularly with improv group, Night Bus, at the Free Association in London.

ADELAIDE WALDROP (INTIMACY/MOVEMENT DIRECTOR)

Adelaide Waldrop is an intimacy director, director, and theatre-maker based in London. She graduated from LAMDA in 2017 with an MA in Directing. As an intimacy director/coordinator her credits include *The Color Purple* (Curve Theatre); *Intergalactic* (Sky One); *The Treatment* (LAMDA) and *Rotterdam* (LAMDA). She has trained with Yarit Dor, Lizzy Talbot, Ita O'Brien, and Claire Warden and is currently an apprentice with Intimacy Directors International (IDI) and IDI-UK. She is Co-Artistic Director of Maude, an ensemble theatre company based in London.

45NORTH (PRODUCER)
www.forty-fivenorth.com

45North is an award-winning company which champions the work of female-identifying and non-binary theatre-makers. Founded in 2018 by Jessica Rose McVay, 45North produces in London, Edinburgh and in 2020 began touring around the world beginning in Australia at FRINGEWORLD in Perth, and Adelaide Fringe. We aim to inspire, surprise, provoke, and, entertain with work by underrepresented and unheard voices.

Led by artists, 45North continues to reinvest in emerging creatives who are beginning and expanding their practices, working to help artists through step-changes in career. In 2020 45North launched our First Draft Commission scheme which will commission five pieces of new work by artists from all theatrical disciplines.

THEATRE 503

Theatre503 is the home of new writers and a launchpad for the artists who bring their words to life. We are pioneers in supporting new writers and a champion of their role in the theatre ecology. We find exceptional playwrights who will define the canon for the next generation. Learning and career development are at the core of what we do. We stage the work of more debut and emerging writers than any other theatre in the country. In the last year alone, we staged 65 productions featuring 119 writers from short plays to full runs of superb drama and launching over 1,000 artists in the process. We passionately believe the most important element in a writer's development is to see their work developed through to a full production on stage, performed to the highest professional standard in front of an audience.

Over the last decade many first-time writers have gone on to establish a career in the industry thanks to the support of Theatre503: Tom Morton-Smith (**Oppenheimer**, RSC & West End), Anna Jordan (Bruntwood Prize Winner for **Yen**, Royal Exchange Theatre, Royal Court and Broadway), Vinay Patel (writer of the BAFTA-winning **Murdered By My Father**), Katori Hall (**Mountaintop**, 503, West End & Broadway – winner of 503's first Olivier Award) and Jon Brittain (**Rotterdam** – winner of our second Olivier Award in 2017). **Doctor Who, The Crown, Killing Eve** and **Succession** are just a few of the programmes 503 alumni have written for this year, as well as productions in theatres all around the country and around the world

THEATRE503 TEAM

Artistic Director	Lisa Spirling
Executive Director	Andrew Shepherd
Producer	Gabrielle Leadbeater
Literary Manager	Steve Harper
General Manager	Molly Jones
Marketing Coordinator	Jennifer Oliver
Literary Associate	Lauretta Barrow
Box Office Supervisor	Daisy Milner
Resident Assistant Producers	Tian Brown-Sampson, Darcy Dobson

THEATRE503 BOARD

Erica Whyman OBE (Chair)
Royce Bell (Vice Chair)
Chris Campbell
Celine Gagnon
Eleanor Lloyd
Geraldine Sharpe-Newton
Jack Tilbury
Zena Tuitt
Roy Williams OBE

MEAT

Gillian Greer

Acknowledgements

Thank you first to Lucy Jane Atkinson and Emily Carewe, for their fearless dedication and support. I owe you everything. Thanks also to all of the organisations who supported me both dramaturgically and emotionally in the writing, developing, programming and financing of this show – Jess McVay and 45North, the National Theatre New Work Department, The Mercury Theatre, the team at VAULT Festival, Clean Break Theatre Company, Soho Theatre and of course to everyone at Theatre503 – Andrew Shepherd, Lisa Spirling, Steve Harper and Lauretta Barrow especially. Thanks to the tireless and often underappreciated script readers who identified this script and saw its potential, and to the innumerable producers and artists who generously gave their time and energy to support the development process of this show in a myriad of ways. Thanks to everyone who donated to our crowdfunder, which made this show accessible to everyone. Thanks to John O'Donovan, Matt Applewhite and Sarah Liisa Wilkinson at Nick Hern Books, to our fearless cast for their openness and bravery and to the design, production and stage management team who have made this mad, messy show possible. The biggest thanks of all go to Chef, for obvious reasons.

G.G.

For Mam and Dad

Characters

RONAN
MAX
JO

Setting

Evening at a low-key but expensive restaurant in Dublin City
Centre. Rustic, with mismatched chairs, quirky candleholders,
maybe synth music.

A Note on Pauses

Gaps between dialogue are rough indications of pauses or
silence in the play. They are not prescriptive, simply what felt
right in the writing.

A forward slash (/) indicates overlapping dialogue.

Words in square brackets [] are unspoken.

A Note on Scene Changes

Changes should be done by the cast and should be chaotic,
greedy, emblematic of all the fear, anger, hunger and want they
feel in the play but can't properly express. Wine should be
gulped, spilt, food scoffed or thrown, maybe the odd thing
smashed if health and safety will allow. By the end of the play
the table should be surrounded by bits of destroyed dinner.

*This text went to press before the end of rehearsals and so may
differ slightly from the play as performed.*

ACT ONE

One

We are a few courses into a meal in a fancy restaurant. MAX *and* RONAN *sit in a glum show of civility, it's clear a bomb's been dropped.* RONAN *picks at his food.*

MAX   There won't be any names
             any identifying
             that's not what –

RONAN   Right.

MAX   This is just a courtesy.
             I thought it
             I thought: Only fair you know.
             Up front.
             In advance.

             I was talkin to my editor you know
             like I was tellin ya
             about delving deeper baring
             a version of myself they've never seen before
             a perspective they've

RONAN   They?

MAX   The people
             who read my stuff my my my
             my followers

             Giving them access to
             my past
             my trauma
             to

RONAN   To me?

MAX   No not to you
         access to to to me

         to what you did to me.

         I just want to tell my story
         talk about my my experience of it
         what it means to be yaknow
         a survivor

RONAN   A survivor of what?
         What did you 'survive'?

MAX   That's what we

         What we call ourselves

RONAN   Who?

MAX   The community of women women who

         Look

         You'll have a pseudonym, switch up the details
         the night in question will be
         I want to keep it vague

RONAN   I can see that

MAX   This is more about empowerment
         about
         reaching out to let others know
         they're not alone, yaknow?

         They're not –

Ronan?

You understand, don't ya?
Surely you –

RONAN   Do I?
         Am I supposed to understand?

MAX   This was just a a a
         a courtesy

         I thought

RONAN   You thought?

MAX   I'm not trying to upset you or
         this is

RONAN   What is it?
         An accusation?

MAX   No
         No Ronan it's
         Jesus I
         I mean you were there Ro
         this isn't exactly breaking fucking news

RONAN   Christ

         Christ I mean

         I thought this was
         I thought we
         I thought we were getting on –

MAX   We are getting on

RONAN   Oh my God

         You're a sociopath

MAX   Ronan!

RONAN   Just how did you see this going exactly?
         Like how did you picture this conversation
         in your mind?

MAX   Well I thought you'd be –

RONAN   Thought we'd have a a civilised discussion over tea
         is that it?

MAX   Well yes actually

         I mean

         Well why are you acting like this is a surprise?

         This is this was
         inevitable

RONAN   Are you seriously here for my blessing?

MAX   Understanding.
         I'd like your
         understanding
         that this is
         necessary.
         Important to me.

         My writing –

RONAN   Your writing?
         You can
         You can write about about trees!
         About the housing crisis or
         the border or
         or your fucked-up relationship with your ma
         I am not material
         fodder not

MAX   You're a part of my life, Ro.
         It's been a part of my life.
         Every day.

RONAN   But it's not true!

         It's not true.

         I didn't

I wouldn't.

I never fucking touched you.

MAX   I'm not here to blacken anyone

RONAN   You do blacken me
          Maxine, when you say these things

MAX   Keep your voice down

RONAN   Throw words around like

          Big words

          Serious words!

MAX   You can't even say it can you?

          Go on.

          Say it.

RONAN   Well why should I have to fucking say it
          I didn't fucking do it!

MAX   You're denying it

RONAN   There's no way out of this.

MAX   You're telling me that it didn't happen?
          That I invented –

RONAN   No matter what I say to this I'm fucked
          it's a trap.

MAX   No

RONAN   I deny it I'm a liar
          I agree with you then I'm I'm I'm

MAX   A good man, Ronan.
         A good man who did a shit thing and I'm just askin
         I'm telling you.
         I need to do this.

         Please.

         This was wrong.
         I shouldn't have

         Shouldn't have come I'm

         She grabs her stuff.

RONAN   Sit down

MAX   Maybe a phone call or or an email would have been

RONAN   No wait Maxine don't go anywhere

MAX   Maybe my agent could talk to

RONAN   Max alright listen if I –

MAX   You know maybe this is more of a solicitors
         situation

RONAN   Jesus just sit the fuck down will ya?

         He entreats her.

         Eventually, she sits back down.

RONAN *goes to speak.*

MAX   I have to piss.

No one moves.

Two

Time travels backwards. The table is cleared, the mess removed.

MAX *and* JO *in the dining room.*

The awkwardness settles.

JO   He'll be along in just a bit.

            MAX *smiles*

            He sends his apologies.
            Service is –

MAX   It's fine

            I know how busy he must be –

JO   Great.

            Any minute now.

            Right through that door he'll be.

            Any minute.

MAX   I really don't mind / waiting

JO   In the meantime I can

I'll be your server for tonight.

Jo.

MAX   Hi Jo.

Max.

JO   I know.

Anything from the bar?

MAX   Oh
Oh no no
Thank you though

JO   Water?

MAX   Um actually –

JO   Still? Sparkling?
Mint and lemon?

Tap?

MAX   Tap water would be great yeah thanks.

JO   No problem.

Be right back.

She exits

MAX *sinks into her seat. Straightens herself up,
checks her reflection in a spoon. She's thrumming
with nerves. People are staring, are people
staring? What is she doing here? This was a huge
mistake.*

JO *re-enters with a jug of tap water and pours.
She deposits a bottle of wine on the table.*

MAX   Thanks.

JO *watches her drink.*

MAX *tries to signal her satisfaction.*

And her discomfort.

JO   Good evening and welcome to MEAT.
          Chef Ronan and the family are so delighted you
          were able to join us this evening.
          MEAT is a culinary exploration unlike –

MAX   Sorry?

JO   Sorry?

MAX   Sorry
          sorry I didn't mean to –

JO   I'm introducing the meal.

MAX   Oh

JO   It's really essential to the concept.

MAX   Oh
          Eh
          Sorry I mean
          Carry on then?

JO   (*Re-orientating.*)
          MEAT is a culinary exploration unlike anything
          you've seen before.
          We can't guarantee your comfort but we can assure
          you that this will be an experience.
          Any aversions or allergies, moral or medical?

MAX   I
          Yeah – um
          cheese
          maybe?

JO   Cheese and all other animal by-products included
          in our menu are crucial to achieving Chef Ronan's
          creative vision. There will be no additions,
          omissions or substitutes. If you don't like it you
          can, as Chef Ronan says, Fuck Off

MAX (*Near-involuntary.*)
     What –

JO   A little joke we have.
     Vegetarian? Fuck off.
     Vegan? Fuck off.

     Hasidic Jew, pescatarian, lactose intolerant –

MAX Fuck off, Fuck off, Fuck off?

JO   That's the spirit.

     Seriously though are you allergic to cheese?

MAX No
     No no it's fine

JO   You know legally you have to inform me

     Health and safety are really up our holes so –

MAX I'm fine
     It's fine.

JO   Okay, great!
     So while we're waiting I thought we'd start you off
     with the Cococciola Pinot Grigio

MAX Oh I couldn't –

JO   We insist!
     On the house.

     For the wait.

MAX I um
     Eh
     Well

JO   It's white wine.

MAX Yes

JO   Very dry.
     Notes of wildflowers and honey.
     Lingering finish.

MAX   Um

           Well, go on then.

           JO *serves the wine sommelier style. Waits for* MAX
           to taste it.

           MAX *swills, sniffs it. She has no idea what she's*
           doing.

           It's eh
           Nicely chilled

JO   I'll bring you out some bread

MAX   No no I'm fine

JO   Oh it's no bother.

MAX   I – I – I won't no –

JO   It's fucking good bread, like

MAX   Right,

           Right I'm sure

JO   Ah you'll have some

MAX   No really I'm fine I

JO   Won't be a second!

MAX   I I I can't stay that long you see I

           But JO*'s long gone.*

           MAX *drinks the wine.*

           A long pause. MAX *breathes. Makes sure she's*
           invisible.

Rape.

Rape.

Rape.

Rape rape rape.

Rape.

Raped.

Raped me.

You raped.

You raped me.

Rape.

She drinks more.

Checks to make sure no other tables have noticed her.

Look I eh
I know this is

A lot

And I'm not mad I'm not

but I just –

I just need –

She reaches for her wine again, as RONAN *enters out of nowhere, in bloodied chef whites.*

RONAN   Howiya gorgeous!

MAX   (*Knocking back wine.*)
         Ronan – hi!

         It's awkward.

         Come here!

         They hug.

RONAN   Here listen, I didn't mean to keep ya waiting –

MAX   Oh you're fine – it's fine.

RONAN   You know I'd never intentionally

MAX   Don't even think of it
         Wine?

RONAN   Thanks.

         MAX *pours them both more wine.*

         They toast one another and drink.

         You look well.

MAX   Thanks.

         You – you look

RONAN   Really glad you got in touch.
         I mean
         It's been a minute yeah?

MAX   Yeah!
         Yeah, it has.

RONAN   It's great to have ya here.

MAX   Yeah
             Yeah

             They drink.

RONAN   Jo lookin after ya alright?

MAX   Oh I just sat down –

RONAN   No ordinary waitress, Jo
             She's the GM, brains behind the operation like.
             Keeps the place from falling down around me.

MAX   I can imagine

RONAN   An honour to be served by her, I'm tellin ya!

             JO *returns with bread.*

JO   Fig and walnut toast with rooftop honey.

RONAN   Aw you need to see it, Maxine.
             Didn't give us planning permission to extend the
             garden so we put one on the fucking roof!
             Organic, sustainable, all that craic.
             Carrots are beautiful, fucking spectacular dill.

MAX   You keep bees? Up there?

RONAN   Bees?

             FUCK bees bees yeah bees
             Jo here's a dab hand with the aul bees ain't ya –

JO   Consider them my contribution to the meal.

RONAN   Has those things trained like dogs she does.
             Don't cross this one or she'll set the swarm after ya

             RONAN *pats* JO *affectionately as she's serving,*
             everyone notices.

JO   (*To* MAX, *re: wine*.)
            Any more Maxine?

MAX   Max.
            Well, it is Maxine but I go by

            This looks GREAT

JO   Well I'm glad you like it.

            Are we ready to order?

MAX   Maybe just a nibble

RONAN   Throw on the works
            No cheese for this one she gets gassy as fuck yeah

MAX   Sorry I

JO   Wouldn't that fly in the face of our 'culinary
            vision'

MAX   That's really good of you but

RONAN   An exception, a small exception

JO   That's how it starts

MAX   Well

JO   First it's small exceptions and next it's cocktail
            sausages and colouring books

MAX   I'm fine, honestly, honestly I'm fine –

RONAN   I love your commitment, I do but

JO   There's a cheese COURSE, Ronan

RONAN   Well we'll skip the fucking cheese course, won't
            we?

MAX   I'm actually up against a deadline, so

RONAN   I'll even let you eat our burrata

JO   I'm not the least bit interested in your burrata

MAX   I REALLY CAN'T STAY FOR LONG
             ACTUALLY.

             Sorry.

             It's just I've got this
             thing
             In the morning and I really have to

             This all looks amazing but

RONAN   It's a restaurant

MAX   Yeah
             I know
             but

RONAN   It's my restaurant

             My brand-new, state-of-the-art, very fuckin fancy
             restaurant and you're not

             You're not eating?

MAX   I
             em
             Sorry
             I guess I didn't

JO   I can do you up something small

             We've these little amuse-bouches that'll change
             your LIFE

RONAN   I will be mortally offended if you do not sample
             this menu

MAX   Of course

Oh my God obviously

sorry, I should have thought

I mean –

Sounds great.

RONAN   Perfect! We'll have the foie gras
the agnolotti
maybe some oysters to start
and we'll take it from there, yeah?

MAX *is like a mouse in a trap.*

MAX   That all sounds
really good [but] –

RONAN   Great!
Glad that's sorted.

And can we get two negronis, and another bottle of
this chilling before –

On a look from JO.

Eh you know yourself.

JO   (*To* MAX.)
How's the wine?

MAX   Oh great it's
you know you really know your –

JO   Yep, I do.

Enjoy that bread now!

Exit JO.

MAX   She's great.

RONAN   Scares the fucking shit out of me.

             She's amazing.

             More wine?

             MAX *nods*.

Three

MAX *and* RONAN *are awaiting their first course.*

RONAN   I hear eh
                congratulations are in order

MAX   Oh

RONAN   A fuckin book!
                With a cover and
                that you can buy in shops and all!

MAX   You eh
                You heard about that?

RONAN   Course I heard about it!
                All them years on that blog paying off

MAX   Still got the blog

RONAN   Must feel amazing.

                To finally feel like a a a a writer!

                A proper one like.

MAX   You'd be surprised the people you can reach with
                my platform.

RONAN   Oh sure

                Sure

MAX   The blog it's as real to me as any

RONAN   There's somethin about the the
                physicality though

                Yaknow?
                the paper, the spine
                the nineteen ninety-nine in Eason's on O'Connell
                Street of it
                the eh...

MAX   Legitimacy?

RONAN   Right
          the weight
          a book it's got –

MAX   It's got weight yeah
          I get it.

RONAN   Yeah.

          Have you a mock-up of it?
          The cover and stuff?

MAX   I mean

          It's not something I've really
          like

          Not my area, yaknow?

          The publishers they've got experts
          know what sells and stuff
          I just sort of
          let them at it.

          Doesn't really matter anyway
          As long as it's got words

RONAN   Are you serious?

          Everything matters.
          EVERYTHING.
          The grade of the paper, the font, the size of the
          thing in your hand.

          If that's shit you've got nothing –

MAX   Ah I don't think –

RONAN   I'm serious Maxine.

          You shoulda seen me when I got this place!
          Obsessed with with

skirting boards wood panelling light fixtures
with the nuts and bolts physical fuckin
manifestation of it
the fact that I could touch it, hold, close open
the door

That it was – real
fuckin floored me
I made sure that everything

EVERYTHING

Went through me. Made it mine.

MAX   Thought you weren't meant to judge a book by its
cover.

RONAN   Listen to me
Nobody knows your vision better than you.

You don't compromise that shit for anyone.

MAX   Even if it gets you in trouble.

In the papers, maybe?

RONAN   Ah that's just

Free publicity, ya know?

Pissin people off gets attention.

MAX   'Vegetarian? Fuck off.
Vegan? Fuck off.

Hasidic Jew, pescatarian, lactose intolerant…'

RONAN   I just got so sick of it.
All the dietaries, the overnight coeliacs
'no gluten soy ok though'
Soy IS gluten for fuck's –
and vegans right, vegans
complainin about the horrors of the dairy industry
one minute
shoving coke up their noses the next

And us lettin them!

The hypocrisy of it like.
All these soft edges
performing concern.
Gluten-free dairy-free almond bollocks.

MAX   Right.

RONAN   It feels like
the whole industry
we've forgotten about the food, ya know?

The thing we're all here for!
Integrity of flavour.
No compromises.

MAX   Mm.

RONAN   And an all-meat menu at least that's
well it feels
Primal, ya know?
Honest.
Straightforward.
No bullshit.

MAX   It's certainly very
You.

RONAN   I mean people eat it up too
We're booked up for – weeks

People say it's

Shockin or whatever but
they love it

They fuckin love it.

MAX   And how's your ma?

RONAN   Oh, deadly
           she's great
           gettin on now, yaknow

           But she's so fuckin proud of me

MAX   I'll bet she is

RONAN   Was askin after ya

           Actually

           Never thought she'd see the day, ha?
           Me, me own place, 'career'

MAX   Tis far from the flats of Crumlin you are now!

RONAN   We heard about

MAX   Oh, Jesus Christ don't / it's fine it's totally fine

RONAN   We were so

           We were so
           sad

           For ya

           Shoulda reached out

MAX   Nah
           Nah sure
           why would ya

           was a long time comin.

           I wrote about it
           on the blog yknow

           At the time.

RONAN   Did ya?

            I eh
            I must have missed that one –

MAX   One of my biggest pieces.
            'Surviving My Mother's Death'
            Alcoholism, you know
            addiction

            Kinda what landed me the book deal
            I think.

            They said I was 'Eloquent in Misery'

            Should thank her really.

            Sorry
            Sorry can we talk about something else?

RONAN   Shit yeah of course

MAX   I think it's better if we

RONAN   Yeah of course yeah

MAX   Don't want to

RONAN   Totally get it

MAX   Maudlin

RONAN   Totally

            Listen em

> *He goes to toast.* MAX *is clearly uncomfortable.*
>
> To us
>
> For fuckin
> provin all the bastards wrong, eh?

MAX   Thanks.

They cheers.

Enter JO.

JO   It's eh

RONAN   Foie gras

On a marmalade brioche

Baked in-house
By me.

JO   You make the stuff I big it up, alright?

RONAN   Whatever you say captain.

MAX   It eh
it looks delicious

JO   Oh it is

May I?

Indicating the bread.

RONAN   Crack on

JO *begins slicing up the brioche, carefully
smearing on the foie gras and serving it up for*
MAX *and* RONAN.

Tell Jo about it then.

MAX   What?

RONAN   The book!
           Come on

JO   Oh please do
           PLEASE do

MAX   Oh eh
           I didn't
           that's not why I'm –

RONAN   Come on Maxine
           We're dyin ta hear.

MAX   You really wanna know?

RONAN   I do

JO   He does.

MAX   Okay.
           So.
           I mean it's meant to be kind of a memoir
           A look back on my life yaknow
           my eh
           tumultuous upbringing

RONAN   Of course

MAX   Um
           Junkie ma
           Feminist awakening

RONAN   Methodone, AA, Activism!

MAX   Right

JO   Burnin bras and takin names!

MAX   Thank you

JO   Absolutely

RONAN   College?

MAX   Some college

JO   Navigating the treacherous patriarchy of academia

MAX   Right

RONAN   Friends, foes, lovers.

JO   Exposing the hypocrisy of the liberal elite

MAX   I hope so

RONAN   Me?
           Us?!

           Do you remember our Midnight Picnic?

           The Midnight Picnic?

           Come on, Maxine!

MAX   Um

RONAN   I just thought yaknow because

           You reminded me.

JO   I'll just
           get a drop more wine, shall I?

RONAN   That'd be lovely

           JO *exits to go get wine.*

           It's stupid.

MAX   What?

RONAN   This is typical me
             Runnin my mouth off when I should be

MAX   Ah well you have to tell me now!

RONAN   No really I am all ears.

MAX   I know you can't keep it in

RONAN   I interrupted you

MAX   Get it out of your system.

             Maybe it'd be good

             For the book, like.

             Go ahead.

RONAN   So you were fucking off.
             I dunno interrailing with 'Caoimhe' or some shite

             Are you still in touch with her?

MAX   Oh, um –
             You mean Cliona?

RONAN   Something
             and it was early days
             for us
             you had the eh eh eh
             the pink hair? With the –

             You looked like one of them troll dolls but cute
             and I was like FUCK
             she's goin to EUROPE
             she's got this HAIR
             she's gonna meet some
             with like a like a man bun
             She's gonna meet a walking talking man bun in
             a tent and forget all about me.

MAX   Oh

RONAN   So I thought
           I'll arrange something
           really grab her attention.
           Something to remember me by – yeah?
           Before you went.

           Are ya

           Are you gonna be writin this down, or?

MAX   Oh
           Oh yeah I mean

           MAX *scrabbles for some way to write the story
           down, pulls out a pen and scrawls on a napkin for
           paper.*

           Ready.

RONAN   So I planned this picnic, yeah?
           Thought I'd do it all from scratch
           wicker basket
           little knives
           the whole thing

           And I was so committed
           I was gonna make you a feast like nothing –
           nothing you had ever seen!

           Had me Jamie Oliver YouTube video all fired up
           Me ingredients
           Me measuring all done out

           I was gonna show you that I was the man who
           who deserved you

           Who could provide

I was gonna spoil ya fuckin rotten.

Well how was I meant ta know that oil was so
fuckin flammable?

MAX *snorts, it's coming back to her now.*

MAX   Oh my God
          Your poor ma

RONAN   Lived on cup-a-soups and Supermacs then, didn't I?
          Didn't know me coriander from me cumin so

MAX   You filled the chip pan to the brim!

RONAN   I was makin TEMPURA

MAX   Was a miracle you didn't bring the whole house
          down

          The whole road!

RONAN   You show up and there's smoke pourin out the
          front door like we're namin a new pope

MAX   Your ma with a fire extinguisher

RONAN   (*Extremely Irish Mammy voice*.)
          'The absolute gowl, he'll kill us all!!'

MAX   'Mind the foam there dear, not on your lovely
          gúna'

RONAN   She loved you

MAX   What a legend.

RONAN   So I had to improvise.
          With very limited supplies

MAX   Rashers!

RONAN   Rashers piled high on the plate

MAX   with cheese, in sandwiches

RONAN   On ice cream!

MAX   Rashers and ice cream!

            I remember!

            Jesus we were fucking rank

RONAN   Delicious!

MAX   Greasy!

RONAN   You were mad for it!
            Rashers for breakfast, dinner and tea

MAX   Well my palette has matured since then

RONAN   We were pioneers!
            Hungry and in love
            Scoffing ourselves stupid on the green outside
            Eamon Ceannt Park

MAX   Rashers tipped in chocolate spread, Jesus Christ

RONAN   I just saw how happy it made ya
            that night.
            Just messin around

            Eating shite out on the green at midnight
            like a pair of fuckin urchins or somethin
            falling in love

            Right on cue, JO *re-enters.*

JO   Wine wine wine for everyone

MAX   Ronan, I –

JO   Get that down ya now
            I've saved this bottle specially

RONAN   And that was the start!
            My eh, journey of self-discovery.

Never would have picked up a spoon if it wasn't for
if it wasn't for that.

MAX   Thanks, Ronan.
           That's
           nice.
           That's really nice

RONAN   Ah I've got a million more where that came from –

JO   You've not touched the food!

RONAN   What?

JO   This stuff is like crack
           It's like his crack

           Not crack like CRACK crack just crack like

           Crack like Delicious

           Crack like Addictive
           I mean –

MAX   I've never had it

RONAN   What? It's amazing

           Eat eat eat eat eat!

           RONAN *goes to feed* MAX *a bite.*

JO   Give the girl some space Ro

           MAX *is able to avoid eating it.*

Do ya know how it's made?

Do ya know like how they make it like?

MAX   Do I

Do I want to?

JO   Aw it's a great story

He loves telling it

RONAN   Maybe not
right now

JO   Ah no you have to tell her
she'll love it

Go on

RONAN   Oh eh

Right.
Right!

As this goes on JO *serves the wine and clears the
table as needed.*

It's
It's liver.

Duck liver it's
it's pure duck liver.

I get it from this guy in Spain
His name's Eduardo and his stuff is famous
world famous like – he's done a TED Talk!

See, most farms

They take their ducks and they put them in these
these cages yeah
and shove these big fuck-off metal tubes down
their necks

force feed them like
till their livers grow stupidly
to stupid sizes

awful stuff

But Eduardo, Eduardo doesn't do that shit

He's got this farm, just acres of the most beautiful
Spanish land you can think of

No cages, no fences, nothing

Doesn't need em.

The ducks love it there.

And Eduardo he loves his ducks too like
He believes ducks are sensitive, intelligent
believes they fall in love, connect with people,
dream

He sings to them, worships them

Gives them the best fuckin lives a duck could
ask for.

And so when the ducks are nice and fat and safe
and happy
he takes the feed, the same feed that the bad farms
use
and he just leaves it around the farm for them to eat
at their little ducky leisure, like.

So the food is just left there out and the ducks
well they go mad for the stuff
it's like high protein high nutrient

JO   it's like crack for ducks basically

RONAN   Right and they eat themselves
          eat themselves fucking silly
          no tubes no torture no nothing
          just happy fuckin ducks and food and patience

so they they they eat the stuff
they eat
and eat
and eat

And eat

And eat

And at the end of what? Two weeks of that they've
eaten so much they can't walk
and now
now they've these massive, beautiful livers just
bulging outta them
and they just
they just die!

Eduardo doesn't even have to kill them

They just keel over and fuckin die and they leave
behind this amazing stuff
and Eduardo well he has a little duck funeral for
them
and he consoles their little duck families

And he slices their livers outta them and sells it on
to me in kilos
and I cook it with thyme and rosemary and spread
it on crackers
and serve it to the rich cunts that come in here.

He probably eats some here

The poor things fuck themselves.

Totally fucking fuck themselves.

MAX *has gone a bit pale now.*

MAX   Excuse me

RONAN   What?

JO   Ah you're alright love don't worry

RONAN   She's gone white

MAX   No no I haven't I'm fine I'm just

             Just a bit sick

RONAN   Your food'll go cold

JO   It's a cold course, Ronan

             Do you need a hand love?
             A Panadol or something?

MAX   No no actually I think I should go home I think

RONAN   But you just got here

JO   Sit down a minute you do look a bit off-colour

MAX   Please don't touch me

JO   I wasn't trying ta

MAX   No no I know I understand it's just

             sorry sorry I just

             This is all great

             Really great but but I

             I need to tell you something.

             The scene dissolves in dance, music and duck liver.
             The bomb goes off.

ACT TWO

Four

JO *is clearing off the second course. It's getting late.* MAX *is away in the bathroom,* RONAN *enters.*

JO   ?

RONAN   She's fine

            Be out in a minute.

JO   Great.

            Good.

            Great.

            RONAN *sits down.*

            She feeling okay?

            Is she – ill is she

            Do we need to call someone / or

RONAN   She's fine
         okay she's fucking fine

         Dandy even

JO   She's not touching the food.

RONAN   Don't know if either of us have much of an appetite
         at this point

JO   That's never stopped you before.

RONAN *puts his head in his hands.*

RONAN   FUCK

Eventually, JO *sits, calm as anything.*

JO   Listen to me very carefully, okay

         You get her out of here in the next five minutes

         or I pull the fucking fire alarm / and close the place
         for the night

RONAN   We can't just throw her out

JO	This is untenable it's an untenable situation
	The punters can hear her, you know?
	And you
RONAN	I'm not saying anything / anything that
JO	booming on about your 'innocence'
	Your 'good name'
RONAN	What am I supposed to do, take it?

Jo

She's calling me a

JO   I know what she's calling you.

RONAN   FUCK

JO   Hey

Hey

A sense they're being watched.

Stop making a spectacle of yourself.

RONAN   This is all they need this is / all they fucking need

JO   You don't think I know / that?

RONAN   Any excuse to tear this place down

To tear me down / they'll take it

JO   I know I know

RONAN   FUUUUUCCCCKKKK

JO   SHUT UP RONAN

            Christ if ya can't

            If ya can't keep it together now well then

            Jesus

RONAN   I won't be smeared

            Dragged through the mud I won't be

JO   You think you're the only one who's in the shit
            with this?

            Christ I mean

            This place belongs to me too to all of us

            You think we want our work destroyed because

            Because of your your your your

            foolishness

RONAN   Ah.

            I see.

JO   No

            No no I never said / that

RONAN   Nah
            Nah you you didn't need to.

Jo.

You know me.
You know I wouldn't

That I would never

Please!

JO   No

No I know.

RONAN *is getting emotional now.*

RONAN   Christ I mean
             I fuckin loved her, you know?

JO   I know you did, Ronan.

They sit in this for a minute.

RONAN   You really think people have heard?

JO   Yes.

             I do.

RONAN   How much?

JO   Enough. The lads can tell something's up.

             They're getting distracted –

RONAN   Fuck the lads

JO   Ronan

RONAN   You know what tell them tell them from me

That paté was gritty as fuck

And they'd want to step it the fuck up if they wanna keep their jobs

He thrusts some bit of leftover food in her direction to send back to the kitchen.

Well go on

Tell them

JO takes it, along with what's left to clear from the table and goes to exit.

Just as she's about to exit, RONAN *breaks down.*

Jo

Jo I'm
Scared I'm scared I'm fucking
scared

He cries desperately.

JO   Right

JO abandons her work and goes to RONAN.

Right it's okay

I have ya.
It's okay.

> *They hold each other for a moment,* RONAN *deep in it.* MAX *enters and sees them.* JO *and* MAX *lock eyes.* JO *gently disentangles herself from* RONAN.

MAX   Hi

Could you get me my coat

please

RONAN   (*Simultaneous.*) Don't do that

JO   (*Simultaneous.*) I think that'd be best.

Don't mind him and don't move

I'll be right back

JO *exits lightning-fast.*

MAX   I want to leave

RONAN   Don't

MAX   You have a legal team, right?

We'll need to exchange information, at some point

RONAN   Not yet okay?

Come here…

MAX   I really think it's best if I –

RONAN   No, really, Maxine I'm serious

Don't leave it like this.

I can't

Leave it like this.

I

I'm not a bad person

MAX   I know that Ronan.

I do.

I wouldn't have come here if I thought –

RONAN   I
I lost the rag with ya I did
I know I did

That's what I do but I

Um

JO *returns with* MAX's *coat and bag.*

If you stay, I'll

If you stay I'll

JO   You'll what?

Ronan?

RONAN   I don't remember that night, alright?

I don't understand

any of this but

But

I want to.

I'm ready to listen.

Hand on heart, Maxine, I swear to fuck I am.

Will you just sit back down with me please so we
can talk?

MAX   I'm putting it in the book, you know

RONAN   I know

MAX   You won't stop me.
             You won't convince me that –

RONAN   Of course not I
             I wouldn't

MAX   I'm not here for your permission.

             I just

             I just want you to hear me out.

RONAN   And I will.

             We will, yeah?

             I swear to you.

             I'm all ears.

             MAX *and* RONAN *sit back at the table.* JO *stands
             with the coat and bag. They look at* JO *as if for
             guidance.*

JO   Right then.

             What you having next, so?

Five

MAX *and* RONAN *are eating pasta. Well,* RONAN *is. Silence is a third character in this scene.*

RONAN   So

MAX   So

RONAN   Are ya gonna

MAX   I'm getting there.

RONAN   Sure sure

             I'm all ears, just so ya know.

             Here and ready to listen.

MAX   I'm working up to it

RONAN   In your own time.

MAX   Yeah

           Yeah
           Good

RONAN   Great

MAX   Great

RONAN   How's the pasta?

MAX   (*Has not eaten*.) Oh it's great

           Great.

RONAN   Good

Whenever you're ready

MAX   Sure.

Y'know, I imagined this a dozen times.

Sitting here

Telling you

Everything.

Giving you a piece of my mind!

RONAN   So why don't ya?

MAX goes to drink, there's no wine left.

MAX   D'ya think I could get some more [wine]

RONAN   Sure, sure

           RONAN signals offstage for wine.

           Somewhere offstage, JO *signals that he may go
           fuck himself.*

So eh

What date was it?

The night in question?

MAX   What?

RONAN   What time?

Surely you have a
like a / record

MAX   It isn't like that

It's not a

It's not a criminal investigation / Ronan

RONAN   No no course not

That'd need what like

Evidence

Or something

MAX   You have no idea how hard this is.

Sitting here in in in your domain your turf and
saying this
all this

To you

Most women never face their abusers / head-on
you know

RONAN   Abusers?

MAX   It's just another term / another

RONAN   Well do ya have a glossary or something

cos I don't speak fuckin Girl Power do I?

Can you just please give me something
anything
any sort of inkling of what you

What you think I did

MAX   You really don't remember, do you?

Sorry

It's just I thought it was obvious I mean I'd
assumed

It's burned into my memory so I thought

Fuck, Ronan, how do you not remember

RONAN   Can't remember what didn't happen now can I?

MAX   That's not fair no / you said you said you'd listen

RONAN   What am I listening to here Max? What do you
have to say?

Cos I'm getting sweet fuck-all so far.

MAX   Christ where is that wine

RONAN stands up, MAX flinches.

He goes to a waiter's station and pulls a bottle of wine.

He uncorks it expertly, serves it to MAX.

Thanks.

MAX tries to swish the wine and drink it as she did in front of JO earlier.

RONAN supresses a giggle.

What's so funny?

RONAN   Aw nothin nothin it's just

Yknow what never mind

Not the time, I think.

MAX   Right.

She sniffs the wine again.

RONAN *laughs again, louder this time.*

Ronan!

RONAN   Sorry, I'm sorry no

It's just cute that's all

MAX   I am so out of my depth here

RONAN   It's fancy as fuck, right?

Wouldn't serve me if I didn't own the place!

RONAN *drinks wine straight from the bottle.*

MAX   Ah now you're just showing off

RONAN   Maybe a little

MAX   God you're

You're just the same old Ronan aren't you?

RONAN   The very same.

MAX   Haven't changed haven't

Grown / up

RONAN   Nah
Never!

MAX   Christ this is so hard!

           I thought you'd be like this businessman now

           Wiser or

           Grander or

           Somethin

           but you're just

           You're just yourself

RONAN   You say that like it's a bad thing

MAX   I mean I want to tell ya I do but

           There's no roadmap for this

           I've no idea how to...

RONAN   I was surprised when ya walked in

           How happy I was to see ya

           To catch up, like

           Maybe we could just do that for a bit

           Just talk

           Like old times

           Maybe it'd

           Help or

           I dunno

           Make this all seem a bit less scary

           I come in peace, you know?

MAX   Yeah

             Me too

             She drinks more wine, incorrectly.

RONAN   Fuck's sake

             Pass me that

             You're makin a show of me.

             MAX *passes* RONAN *the bottle of wine.*

             RONAN *swills the wine and holds it up to the light.*

             See that? They're the legs

             That's for alcohol

             See how it clings to the sides of the glass

             Basically means this shit is lethal

             Fifteen to sixteen per cent easy

             Now smell it

             Really get your nose in there

             No really

             Fuckin

             In there

             You smell it?

             MAX *smells it.*

MAX   Yeah

             I

             I think so?

RONAN   You're lookin for three things, okay?

             Fruit, earth, wood

Go again

MAX *smells the wine deeply.*

You got it

Now you gotta aspirate over it

Like this

RONAN *sips the wine noisily, like he's blowing bubbles into it.*

MAX *attempts, dribbles it down herself.*

Ah now come on
you can do better than that

He repeats, MAX *tries to copy him.*

They both slurp at the wine.

Beautiful
Beautiful

They are both getting the giggles now, it's silly and warm.

MAX   I'm getting

Notes of wildflowers and honey

Lingering finish

RONAN   Bingo

Right on the money

They blow bubbles in the wine a little more.

MAX *accidentally sprays some in* RONAN*'s face.*

They both laugh.

MAX   Oh my God

RONAN   Take it easy Maxine

MAX   I'm so sorry let me

RONAN   No problem no problem at all

MAX   Let me help you with that

She wipes his face with a napkin.

RONAN   Truce?

Six

Some time has passed. A fairly elaborate set of a half-dozen oysters has been served. A lot more wine has been drunk. We get the sense of a sort of ceasefire.

RONAN *slowly demonstrates eating an oyster.* MAX *is not impressed.*

MAX   Ronan that looks
            rank

RONAN   Aah you're missin out
            Delicious!

MAX   Thought you'd be above all this craic

            Fancy pesce shit with notions

            He knocks another one back, getting drunk on the decadence of these oysters.

RONAN   Aaaaah

            MAX *is laughing now.*

MAX   Fuck off

RONAN   What?

MAX   Nothin

RONAN   Since when do you not eat seafood anyway?

MAX   Oh it's

            Nothing just

            Like an intolerance or something

RONAN   What you mean like an allergy

MAX   No no no

RONAN   Legally you have to tell us
            Health and safety are so far up our holes that –

MAX   No. I know.

It's fine.

Honestly.

RONAN   Used to love a chipper

         Cod
         Bitta batter

MAX   Well this isn't exactly…

RONAN   What?

MAX   Nothing it's just

         I just

         Never imagined you

         Oysters are just so
         so

         Posh!

RONAN   I'm posh?

MAX   A little bit

RONAN   Jesus if I'm posh you're the fuckin aristocracy

MAX   Ah would ya stop

RONAN   (*Taking the piss*.)
         Going for one at The Shelbourne with the lads
         from the rugby team
         Taking meetings in Avoca before brunch in The
         Happy fuckin Pear

MAX   I'm from the very same road as you Ronan

RONAN   Yeah but you left.

MAX   Yeah
            I know.

RONAN   Your accent's gone mad, ya know

MAX   (*Warmly.*)
            Has it?

RONAN   All them rounded vowels. 'Sh' sounds.

MAX   What 'sh' sounds!

RONAN   Roysh – (*Meaning 'right'.*)

            Washer – (*Meaning 'water'.*)

MAX   I don't talk like that

RONAN   'loike thash'

MAX   How dare you!

RONAN   Just callin it as I see it
            I woulda thought you'd be mad for these y'know?
            You and Caoimhe and Fiach
            Sunday brunch in Howth
            Oysters and prosecco

MAX   Well I'm not okay?

            I'm not like that

RONAN   Right

          Right

          Of course

          .

          (*Eventually, desperately.*)
          Yknow what I love about oysters?

          They're fucking honest.

          No bullshit like

          I don't cook them, yknow?

          don't boil them fry them nothing

          they're just

          plucked right out of the sea and sent to me

          fresh

          true

          just like this.

          Maxine, they're not even fuckin dead yet!

          They're a livin
          pulsin
          breathing thing

that tastes like

like

nothing

you've ever had before in your life.

People say oysters taste like salt or sand or water or
whatever shit but they're wrong

An oyster tastes like the sea it was plucked from
the very moment it was plucked from it.

Its purest essence

The – truth of it.

The soul.

An oyster taken from the Pacific in the height of
summer
will taste nothing like one sat in the Atlantic in the
middle of a storm.

It can't
because it's something something

bigger

than that

They're not posh.

Maybe posh is something they've become but

It's not who they are

Not the core of the thing.

Inside they're

they're fucking

Godly.

He toasts her with an oyster and knocks another one back.

MAX *is kind of floored.*

MAX   That's

           That's beautiful.

RONAN   Too fucking right it is.

MAX   Can I have one?

           An oyster, I mean

           Suddenly have

           Like a craving

RONAN   What about your
           intolerance?

MAX   I think I'll live.

           RONAN *nods.*

           He takes an oyster and goes to feed it to MAX.

           They are very close.

RONAN   Can I?

MAX   Yeah

           Yeah

           RONAN *gently goes to tip* MAX's *head back and feed her the oyster.*

           They are interrupted at the last second when JO *enters to clear the table.*

JO   How are we gettin on?

MAX and RONAN *look at one another, frozen briefly in their closeness.*

The scene dissolves, they knock back oysters greedily, which turn into shots. They get blackout drunk.

Seven

A little later. They are sat back down again. RONAN *is ravenously attacking his food.* MAX *is reading from a slim set of pages.* RONAN *braces himself.*

RONAN   Okay go

MAX   It was at a party.

           In some
           tricked-out mini-mansion out in Booterstown

           He was drunk.
           We both were.

           We loved one another but I could feel it
           curdling

           It's strange how envy can manifest

           It's like an ache
           a throb that eminates from his whole being

           For the first time in a dim, adolescent memory
           I was happy

           and it killed him.

           RONAN *shifts, uncomfortable.*

           I heard it first before I registered the blood
           He had smashed something
           thrown it

           a Waterford Crystal vase singing across the room
           and crashing down
           landing nowhere in particular

           As pained and aimless as his fury

           We are brushed into an empty room
           A houseful of whispers conscious of our
           movements

the backwater kids from the west side of the city
our un-belonging made manifest

I bandage his cut hand and try to erase what has
happened.

The glances I might have stolen in the wrong
direction
the notions I had gained above my station.

I make myself so small that I might fit in the palm
of his hand.

I wrap myself up in him

I kiss him –

RONAN   (*A breakthrough.*)
         HA!
         You kissed me!

MAX   I'm not finished –

RONAN   came on to me /

         All sexy

MAX   I didn't know how else to to to
         to get through to you

RONAN   You initiated!
         You definitely fucking initiated.
         Consented to

MAX   Not to what happened.
         I never consented to –

RONAN   This is wank

MAX   It's the truth

RONAN   Yeah but not like that
         Yeah those are the things that happened but
         it's not
         those words they

         They twist it all up

MAX   Well how would you describe it

RONAN   We were pissed!

MAX   You wrecked the gaff!

RONAN   It was a gaff party!
             Wreckin was a prerequisite

             Don't leave your fuckin Ming family heirloom
             china shit out if you wanna have a gaff party

MAX   You embarrassed me / in front of my friends

RONAN   and I didn't 'throw' shit
             by the way

             You make it sound like I wanted to cause trouble
             like I did it intentionally

MAX   Well didn't you?

RONAN   No.
             Never.

MAX   They were our friends

RONAN   YOUR friends.

             Your fuckin jet-ski weekend-in-Calais gluten-free
             socialism-lite fuckin friends
             Those friends

MAX   My friends who cared about me
             gave a shit, Fiach…

RONAN   Ah Fiach, Fiach, fucking Fiach!

             I broke a glass, Maxine!

             I broke a glass at a house party.

             You're tellin me that just because 'Fiach' wears
             a blazer
             cos he reads Joyce and listens to The fuckin Smiths

That he hasn't done stuff
worse stuff than that?

that he's not an arsehole?

MAX   That's not what I'm saying

RONAN   What are you saying Max?

I'm serious

Because

I am completely in the fuckin dark here

We… yknow! (*He means fucked.*)
Like always

Like normal.
Maybe I was drunk or annoyed or
Maybe Caoimhe's bathroom wasn't the ideal –

MAX   Cliona's –

RONAN   It doesn't fucking matter

RONAN snatches the manuscript from MAX's hands.

She reacts instantly.

Just tell me, yeah

MAX   Ronan please

RONAN   Just look me in the eyes and and say it

MAX   Give me that back I

RONAN   Just fucking drop the influencer shit and tell me what I fucking did to you

He folds up the pages and tucks them into his chef whites.

Please.

MAX   Alright

So um
I remember having fun.
I remember being sat on a windowsill
with Fiach

RONAN   Oh Fiach

MAX   Talking about the banking crisis, about

RONAN   That's not even a full name, it's a sound

MAX   And I felt
I dunno what it was but I felt
Like I could say what I liked
be who I liked.

RONAN   What you felt was money.
Money and
self-importance.

MAX   I remember
I remember Fiach asking me about the blog and
you

RONAN   Pretending to ask
Feigning interest in

MAX   He was a fan
a supporter he
and this was
this was really early on
Before any of the success or the

RONAN   He was cranin to look at your arse the whole time.

         How is it possible that you're so wilfully fuckin
         naive?

MAX   You're deflecting

RONAN   I mean don't get me wrong

MAX   Trying to distract me

         I can't I can't think if

RONAN   The blog
         everything you were doing
         it was amazing

MAX   Then why hadn't you read it?

RONAN   I dunno

MAX   Ronan –

RONAN   I dunno I dunno I just

         Couldn't

         So?

MAX   I remember you were bleeding
         you cut your hand

         Trying to clean up the glass I think

         I remember the embarrassment

         The absolute nightmare flush of mortification of it

         Of thinking just one night
         couldn't you have given me just one night?

         I remember apologising to Fiach

RONAN   I didn't do anything

MAX   I was furious and you just didn't seem to notice or
         care or
         just kept on and on about being accused

And how they were all just cunts who didn't
understand us
and I wanted to calm you down so so I kissed you

To shut you up more than anything else to be
honest.

And that was when you
grabbed me.
Up against the door

I could feel the handle in the small of my back I

We were close already in that tiny room
You didn't need to

Didn't have to

Yes I had kissed you I did cos I thought it would

Would

Would

I don't know

Help?

Calm ya down maybe?

Fuck's sake

And I then I tried to talk I tried to

And you shushed me

I remember that cos there were people
there were people outside people listening
to the fight and then and then your hand

your hand was on my mouth and I remember this

cos the feel of it was sort of
strong?

It felt
too sure too

Like you weren't touching me

weren't holding me the way you usually
like normal, you know?

So eh
so the handle of the door's against my back and

your hand is on my mouth and I can hear people
outside

and at this point I'm thinking okay

Make sure he doesn't get any blood on your face

Cos you're still bleeding remember

And that's the last thing we need

Everyone already thinks we're

I mean imagine if we walked out of here and

So

I sort of gently move your hand away

And then you

You eh

You unzip your jeans and

RONAN   Ah no

MAX   And you know in that moment I felt

RONAN   Ah no fuck this for a bag of chips

MAX   You know they say it's fight or flight but in that
          moment I just stopped yknow I just /

          STOPPED

RONAN   You unzipped them

          You did

MAX   I thought you didn't remember?

             Ronan?

RONAN   It's coming back to me I I I remember

             Some
             things

             Look you didn't exactly / stop you just stood there

MAX   I think that's what I thought I had to do to keep
             a handle on the situation
             We were already the big drama of the night and
             I didn't want to add any more

             I just thought
             get it over with yknow

             And you know
             I think you wanted them to know.

             I think you wanted Fiach to know

             you needed the whole house to know that I was
             YOURS

             Yours to fuck whenever you wanted

             so I just stood there with my back against the door
             and you fucked me

RONAN   Yeah and you took it!

Instantly regretting this.

Well didn't you?

Said it yourself you you you didn't say anything

didn't stop me didn't

Look I know for a fact that you were the one who unzipped my jeans I I

I'm sure of it

I mean why else would I have

How would I

Maxine how was I meant to know I had to stop?

Enter JO *to clear the plates, bottle of wine at the ready.*

JO   Well

Any more for any more

Senses the tension in the room.

MAX   I didn't want to get you into trouble.

MAX *is close to tears*.

RONAN   and did you fuck him?

MAX   What?

RONAN   After?

           Fiach

           MAX *stands up*.

MAX   Don't ask me that

           RONAN *stands up*.

           Don't take it there

RONAN   To teach me a lesson
           to get back at me?

           While you were

           Stewing about that night

Telling your little friends

Turning everyone against me

Did you fuck him?

MAX   Yeah.

Yeah I did.

RONAN *considers this.*

JO *entreats* RONAN.

RONAN *lets out a roar of frustration, and flips the table.*

Time stands still, then leaps forward.

RONAN *roars at* MAX, JO *jumps between them.*

Customers begin to file out of the restaurant, maybe JO *pleads with them to stay.*

The restaurant empties out.

RONAN *despairs.*

The restaurant folds in on itself.

Everything is truly fucked.

ACT THREE

Eight

We are sucked back in time – right to the beginning of the night.

JO is setting tables for customers. Maybe plays some music on her phone. Dances?! Whatever she does, it's clear she's in her element – this is her favourite part of the day.

Enter RONAN. *He creeps up behind, surprises her with affection.*

JO	Fuckin hell man
RONAN	Howiya gorgeous
JO	Fuck off will ya
RONAN	Ah don't worry they can't see
JO	The servers they
RONAN	Just put out staff food, didn't I?
	Stuffin themselves back there
	They wouldn't notice if a bomb hit the place.
	C'mere
JO	Ah will you ever stop
RONAN	Hello to you too
JO	Do ya not have Something to chop or
RONAN	Any word yet?

JO   You know there's not been

RONAN   Just makin sure

JO   We don't open for another hour

RONAN   I know I know I just

> RONAN *trails off,* JO *goes back to setting the place up.* RONAN *decides to help, but it becomes clear quickly he's more in the way than anything.*

> I love this bit

JO   Me too

RONAN   Just before it all kicks off
            kitchen all set and ready to go

            Peace and quiet

JO   Sometimes.

RONAN   Oi!

> *They wrestle a bit, it's playful.*

> How many covers?

JO   Enough.

            Keep us going.

            Tuesday.

RONAN   Right right.

            Put her on your section yeah

            Near the pass

            I want her to see

JO   I know I know

RONAN   It's just she needs ta

JO   You've told me

RONAN   I want her to see / the

JO   Jesus Christ, Ronan, I know!

            You want to rub your posh ex-girlfriend's nose in it
            you've been perfectly clear

RONAN   Ah
            I can't help it, can I?

JO   Anyone'd think you were looking forward to it

RONAN   I am looking forward to it!

            Showing her what we've built!

JO   What she's missing, ha?

RONAN   She never saw anything in me, you know.

            Never supported me
            never believed

            Dropped me like a hot stone as soon as I left
            college

When I wasn't gonna be a fuckin

Molecular biologist

You know she / filled out my CAO for me

JO   Filled out your CAO for you I know I know

Thought you'd be / 'scientifically minded'

RONAN   'Scientifically minded', Christ

Followed that girl blindly I did

And the minute

The second I started thinking for myself she

You know I bet she thought I'd be half dead in a ditch by now

JO   I'm sure that's not true

RONAN   It is true!

God's honest truth, Jo, I promise you.

Any dietaries in?

JO   Nah
I think most people know the score by now

Word gets around.

Someone rang up and accused us of 'pig genocide' but other than that

RONAN   What's the spread like? Any major pushes?

JO   Eight o'clock-ish looking pretty hairy

             A rake of two tops

             They'll be out by the time she gets here.

RONAN   Right.

             Right.

             I just want –

JO   You want to prove how far you've come, I know.

RONAN   I want to show her that she was wrong

             She was so fuckin wrong

             About me about everything

JO   I think she knows that.

             Why else would she come here?

             JO *and* RONAN *share a look.*

RONAN   I love you

JO   For Christ's sake

             Ronan

RONAN   No seriously
             I've thought about it and

             I love you

JO   You love pints
             You love chips and socks with little pictures of
             rashers on them

             You love –

RONAN   And you!

             For seeing this in me
             For havin faith

JO   I can't go over this again right now

RONAN   We make an amazing team
          We made this place

          All this

          We fuck excellently

JO   One time

          That was ONE TIME

RONAN   I mean imagine – if

JO   This is a professional relationship Ronan

          strictly professional

RONAN   Ah you're no craic

JO   And you never give up, do ya?

RONAN   Nope!

JO   Look

          We've built this place!
          This amazing place I mean

          what more do you want Ronan –

RONAN   Everything

          I want everything.

JO   Fuck's sake.

RONAN   You and me.

          Pioneers! Hungry and in love.

JO   You are embarrassing.

RONAN   Ah

          You love it

          And you know what? She kind of does.

          Some noise or indication of activity from offstage

JO   Here they come.

          G'wan get out of here.

          What're you eyeballin me for?
          Get your hole behind that pass yeah?

          Ronan!

RONAN   I love you

JO   Prick.

          We'll talk later.

          Go on!!

          Giddily, RONAN *bounds offstage. Maybe smacks*
          her arse with a tea towel on the way out.

Nine

We are back to the present.

JO *surveys the mess, a bucket and Marigolds in hand.* RONAN *and* MAX *are on opposite sides of the room.* MAX *has her coat and bag.*

JO   Children

That's what you are

You're a pair of children

RONAN   She started it

JO   You do not speak
do not blink
don't even breathe near me tonight Ronan

JO *passes* MAX *the Marigolds and bucket.*

I have a kitchen to clean down and staff to send home

You – (*To* RONAN.) right that table
I want this place gleaming by the time I get back

RONAN   Jo

Jo ya can't –

JO   Watch me.

You'd do well to remember your place here, Chef.

I'll be back shortly.

Exit JO.

MAX and RONAN *sit in silence for a bit.* MAX
starts to put the gloves on.

RONAN *goes to right the table but struggles.*

It's surprisingly heavy.

Eventually –

RONAN   Sorry

          If you could

          Could you give me a hand here?

          With this?

MAX   I'd really rather not

          RONAN *struggles a bit more.*

          It's really not shifting.

RONAN   Maxine

          Come on

          You've got those weirdly strong arms.

          Please?

MAX   Fuck's sake

She goes to the table, together with a bit of negotiating, they set it right.

RONAN   Thanks.

MAX   Fine.

RONAN starts to clean the mess.
Eventually MAX follows his lead.

RONAN   So eh

What happens with it now then?

The book?

MAX   You know
I have a real rager of a headache right now and I'm really not comfortable

talking

RONAN   Oh

          Sure sure

          Right

MAX   It goes to print
          soon, really soon

          And then it comes out, hardback

          I do a small press tour

          Then who knows?

RONAN   And eh

          What's my pseudonym?

          Look
          Just please don't make it 'Anto'
          Or 'Johnboy'
          Or somethin
          alright?
          I'm beggin ya

MAX   Don't think you've earned a pseudonym

          Do you?

RONAN   No

No of course not

I flipped a fucking table over after all

This sits somewhere between sinister and funny for a little bit too long.

MAX   I didn't think you had it in ya

RONAN   Neither did I

To be honest

MAX   Is she really gonna make me clean this up?
It's your fault

That's gotta be
like
against the Geneva Convention or something

RONAN *laughs.*

What?

What?

It's not funny!

RONAN   You're still pissed

MAX   No I'm not
I'm really fuckin not
actually

RONAN   Nah nah nah I know those eyes anywhere
you're fuckin fluthered

MAX   You flipped a table over!

RONAN   I did yeah

Eventually, they laugh.

You have to admit it was kinda impressive

MAX   Shut up

RONAN   He-Man: Master of the Universe!

MAX   Did you see the way they cleared out?

RONAN   It's all part of my plan, refining my Passionate Chef
persona

MAX   Flying into mad rages at customers

RONAN   We'll say you insulted my vision

MAX   I did insult your vision!

RONAN   Well there you go!

MAX   It's crass and unnecessarily combative

RONAN   That's it

MAX   It's bad for the planet!

RONAN   Yes, let it out Maxine

MAX   AND it's gimmicky as fuck

          RONAN *flings a piece of food at* MAX, *ideally
          something wet. Even more ideally, it smacks her
          right in the face.*

RONAN   That's takin it too far alright?

Maxine?

Ah
Maxine
I'm sorry I was only –

Suddenly, MAX *gets* RONAN *back, good and proper.*

Fuck

You little –

It escalates.

It escalates and escalates and escalates.

It bursts into a full-on food fight.

The two of them are hurling slop across the room at one another, ducking, dodging, throwing chairs, and all the while laughing, laughing, really bloody laughing.

Eventually in the madness, RONAN *grabs* MAX. *There's a strange feeling of déjà vu – we've been here before.*

A hundred years pass in a single second.

And for that second, it all goes away

For a second, it all makes sense.

For a second, everything is fixed.

MAX *and* RONAN *kiss, and it's absolutely terrifying.*

Don't – don't move.

RONAN *exits.*

Ten

MAX*'s head is spinning following the kiss.* JO *appears
seemingly out of nowhere.*

JO   So how much are you getting for it.

MAX   Sorry?

JO   This this
             book.

             How much?

MAX   I

             Sorry I

             I I I don't
             have to

             explain myself to you I –

JO   Good money was it?

             Considering

MAX   Why is that relevant?

JO   Think I have a right to know at this stage, don't you?

MAX   Dunno.

           Depends really on sales
           and reprints and

JO   But there must have been like an advance, right?
           To write it?
           A fee?

           How much?

MAX   Well why does it matter

JO   S'pose it doesn't.

           Just

           You could have written about this any time
           anywhere.
           You've had that blog
           how long?

           Why now?

           Musta been at least
           ten grand right?
           Maybe twenty?

           With your following.

           Was there a bidding war for you?

           You'd given your ma away to them for free so what
           was he?
           Exclusive content?

MAX   This is my story I I I

JO   Yes yes of course you're right it is
            it is
            your 'story'

            I've got stories too, yknow.

            Stories'd turn your blood to ice.

            Long nights in hot kitchens filled with furious,
            frustrated, stupid men

            Men who'd dip your hand in boiling oil if you so
            much as dropped a cheque

            Men who'd leave marks on you

            Proper villains like

            I wonder if you'd like to hear them?

MAX   If that's true
            you should leave, you know?
            Get out start your own place / you know I could –

JO   Are you stupid?

            Ronan's not one of those men.

MAX   No

            Sure
            I I knew that.

JO   There is so much
            dark
            out in the world.

            That you've never even fucking encountered.

MAX   I'll rewrite it
             I will I'll be honest and clear
             about Fiach about

             I won't come out of this snow white you know

JO   No

             No I'm sure your followers will relate to how
             flawed you are

             The mistakes you made along the way

             You don't feel anything

             You're a fucking sociopath

MAX   Well maybe that's right

             Maybe I am
             yknow?

             Cos I don't think about it!

             Not as much as you'd think I do
             Not as much as you'd expect

             I'd forgotten, to be completely honest with you
             For years

             Well not forgotten exactly just
             Not fully thought it through

             Like it was from another life, you know?

             In the face of my ma and
             everything else
             A dodgy college party seemed
             So small

             It was only when my editor, she –
             well I was
             struggling
             I was struggling let's be honest with the book and

There must be something, she said
some other corners of your life
some unexplored

Trauma.
That was the word she used, trauma
You know like blunt force to the head
A wound or something.
Trauma.

A bad ex-boyfriend, maybe?
Assault, Abuse.

No, I said.
No no nothing like that.

Except, that One Weird Night

That's all it was it was
weird
weird and shitty and half-forgotten and
maybe a little sinister in hindsight
maybe a bit fucking
grim
in hindsight

and when I think about it I want to have a long
shower
when I think about it I want to lock myself in
a dark room and scream for a bit
when I think about it I feel gross and used and
ashamed but

but the truth is I don't think about it.

I don't pour out my cornflakes in the morning
thinking about rape
Haven't closed myself off from the world
Haven't stopped loving or living
I haven't been broken by it.

So yeah maybe I am a fuckin sociopath

But I'm also right.

I I I
I know I am.

Enter RONAN, *fizzing with energy. He presents
something to* MAX *with a flourish – a wildly
elaborate ice-cream sundae.*

RONAN   Do you remember?

MAX   Oh my God

Is that –

RONAN   Rashers and ice cream

Known in the world of haute cuisine as the bacon
sundae.

Highlight of the menu

my masterpiece.

MAX   You still make this?

RONAN   Perfected them.

Ice cream mixed by hand right here, rendered
bacon fat, candied rashers, walnuts

You do remember

MAX   Ronan, I –

RONAN   All those late nights with nothing in the house and
us starving throwing shit together
experimenting

MAX   Pioneers

RONAN   Hungry and in love.

I have never once stopped thinking about you.

MAX   I didn't want much you know

I didn't want your blessing or or your friendship or anything
any of this

I just wanted to know I wasn't crazy
that I didn't I didn't dream it or

That it actually happened

And you couldn't even give me that

Could you?

I know you've thought about that night
I know you have

About who unzipped what and when and how

I know you know what happened

That it's stayed with you too

That it was
wrong

RONAN   Maxine will you just

have this with me

Please

I I I dunno what you want me to say

MAX   Yes you do

Yes

You fucking

DO

RONAN

RONAN   Maxine I

I can't do that

JO   You must be hungry

            You've barely eaten all night

MAX   I'm not

            Not a big meat eater

            Recently

JO   What are you one of those vegans

RONAN   Maxine

            Please

            RONAN *holds the bowl out like it's his very heart.*

            MAX *takes the bowl and tastes it.*

            It is delicious.

            It tastes like home.

            MAX *eats.*

JO   Alright

            MAX *eats.*

            MAX *eats.*

MAX *eats and eats and eats.*

It's clear this isn't agreeing with her.

That's enough

MAX *eats.*

RONAN *tries to prise the bowl away from her but she doesn't let go.*

She's got weirdly strong arms.

She eats until she's stuffed.

She eats until she can barely breathe.

She eats until she feels disgust.

She eats through the disgust.

She eats, she eats, she eats.

Ronan, get her to stop

She gnaws and slurps, gulps and chews

RONAN   I'm trying

Maxine!

RONAN *wrestles* MAX *to the ground, she's gone full feral now.*

He tries to stop her, but she won't be pulled off.

She eats

She eats

She eats

She eats

She eats

Until eventually

She vomits.

Eleven

MAX *has vomited everywhere, she's on the floor, retching, sobbing, just generally in bits.*

JO *and* RONAN *look on in shock.*

A long silence.

RONAN	Fuck
JO	Jesus
RONAN	Fuck
RONAN	Christ
	Maxine
	Maxine are you
MAX	Ronan
RONAN	Ohh fuck
JO	Ah look Jesus love
	Don't worry
	Don't you worry one bit okay
	It happens It happens to the best of us
RONAN	Fuck Jo
JO	There now darling
	You're fine
	Everything's going to be fine
RONAN	Jo is she alright is she gonna be alright Jo

Maxine

Maxine I'm sorry I'm sorry I'm so sorry

Maxine can you hear me?

MAX *is drifting in and out of consciousness.*

JO   Okay Ronan I'm gonna need you to get me some
            smelling salts from the first-aid kit

RONAN   The first-aid kit

            The first-aid kit
            Where's the first-aid kit?

JO   In the kitchen

RONAN   The kitchen
            okay

            Yeah yeah yeah yeah yeah

            Dazed, RONAN *runs off stage to the kitchen for
            smelling salts.*

JO   (*To* MAX.)
            Okay sweetheart you're okay you're you're okay

            MAX *stirs, maybe retches a bit.* JO *comforts her.*

            A weight lifts.

            JO *gets up to retrieve a bottle of wine. She settles
            back down next to* MAX *and drinks from the bottle.
            Pours some water for* MAX.

            Here

            You're dehydrated.

            MAX *reaches for the wine.*

Haha very funny

Passes her the water.

MAX *sips tentatively.*

JO *gets a wet wipe and washes* MAX's *face.*

It's lovely.

Suppose I should thank you

For not eating I mean

Means I don't have to scrub half-digested foie gras
out of the grouting

MAX *laughs, weakly.*

You're gonna be fine.

Just fine.

JO *gently wipes the vomit out of* MAX's *hair.*

MAX   Mmm
nice.

The two are quiet for a moment, as JO *tends to*
MAX.

JO *goes to her station and retrieves her secret
stash – a small tray of honeycomb, a can of
whipped cream and two spoons. Maybe sprays the
cream directly in her mouth.*

She offers MAX *a spoon.*

MAX *takes it.*

JO   You know what this is?

Honeycomb.

Fresh from the bees on the roof.

My bees.

Do vegans eat honey?

Don't
actually

Don't answer that.

I don't wanna know.

Well,
if it makes any difference, I treat my bees very well.

My bees.

My little lads.

Course they're all lady bees. The ones that do the
work, anyway.

She tastes a bit of honeycomb.

FUCK me that's gorgeous.

It's basically like a really really intense honey.

It's wax but not 'waxy', if that makes sense?

They make it in these little hexagons to store
pollen in.
And honey

And eggs

It's basically the foundation for their entire life.

It's a ball-ache for them to make.

They need to make and eat like

ten pounds of honey

To get the energy to make basically a drop of this
stuff.

It's their work.

It's their home.

It's everything to them.

And that's what makes it so delicious.

JO tries to feed MAX a bit of honeycomb and cream on a spoon.

It probably took twenty bees

Weeks

To make this much honeycomb?

All those little wings buzzing

Mouths chewing

These clusters of little women killing themselves

And for what?

For us to gobble their lives up with a bit of cream on a spoon?

So fragile, don't ya think?

She dabs a bit of cream on MAX's nose.

MAX   Some life.

JO   Some life.

MAX   I'm sorry

       About

JO   Shut the fuck up.

MAX   I know

       I get that if you know him if you

Care about him

That you might not believe me –

JO   Oh
            fuck I mean

            I believe you.

MAX   You do?

JO   Course I do.

            I mean, come on, have you met him?

            He's a lad

            A thick-as-shit lad who's never known

            Was never taught how ta

            Do I believe that our Ronan did a stupid fucking
            thing to his girlfriend when he was nineteen years
            old and sad and pissed?

            Yeah

            Yeah course I do.

MAX   Okay.

            Okay.

RONAN *bounds back on stage with a bunch of containers of salt – table salt, kosher salt, sea salt, Himalayan pink salt, all things that are very much not the first-aid kit.*

RONAN   I couldn't find the first-aid kit but these are salts

Every kinda salt I could fuckin find

D'ya think that'll –

JO   She's fine, Ronan.

She's just fine.

RONAN *breathes a sigh of relief.*

He comes downstage to sit with the women.

They sit in uneasy peace for a minute.

RONAN   Well that was fuckin

Rank

Everything softens, just a bit.

I have, you know

Thought about it.

That night.

And I never knew why
could never
put my finger on it
on what went wrong

but

I know that
something

went
wrong.

I'm makin a mockery of this now but

I'm just trying to say that that that

You're not crazy, Maxine.

You're not crazy.

MAX   (*Overwhelmed, an implosion.*)
Thank you.

She sinks into JO*'s lap and cries as the weight of*
RONAN*'s words washes over her.*

RONAN *paces upstage as it sinks in for him too.*

JO   Can I ask?

Real talk, yeah?

Why did you come here?

Why did you even need his permission to

Say what you needed to say?

RONAN *takes out the manuscript and starts to*
read it to himself upstage

MAX   I thought

           This was gonna be

           Was meant to be

           Looking him in the eye and

           Speaking my truth would be

           Healing.

           I suppose.

JO   Oh yeah?

           Do you feel healed?

           A quiet moment. MAX *sobs softly into* JO*'s lap.*
           JO *strokes her hair.* RONAN *reads.*

           The restaurant starts to stitch itself back together.

           End of play.

A Nick Hern Book

Meat first published in Great Britain as a paperback original in 2020 by Nick Hern Books Limited, The Glasshouse, 49a Goldhawk Road, London W12 8QP, in association with Emily Carewe, 45North and Theatre503, London

Meat copyright © 2020 Gillian Greer

Gillian Greer has asserted her right to be identified as the author of this work

Cover image by Madison Clare

Designed and typeset by Nick Hern Books, London
Printed in the UK by Mimeo Ltd, Huntingdon, Cambridgeshire PE29 6XX

A CIP catalogue record for this book is available from the British Library

ISBN 978 1 84842 952 9

www.nickhernbooks.co.uk

facebook.com/nickhernbooks

twitter.com/nickhernbooks